Vuyo Maqubela

...BECAUSE I AM WOMAN

Copyright © 2018 Vuyokazi Nomso Maqubela

All rights reserved. No part of this publication may be reproduced, stored in a retrieval system, or transmitted in any form or by any means, electronic, mechanical, photocopying, recording, or otherwise, be lent, re-sold, hired-out, or otherwise circulated without express written consent of the author.

Published by RedOystor Books
an imprint of RedOystor Media (Pty) Ltd

visit www.redoystor.com for more information
Or contact us at **www.redoystor.com/contact-us**

www.redoystor.com/i-am-woman
www.facebook.com/Vuyo_Maqubela
www.instagram.com/Vuyo_Maqubela

Cover Design & Layout by **RedOystor Media (Pty) Ltd**

Printed by **novus print**, a Novus Holdings company

Available on Kindle and other retail outlets

ISBN: 978-0-9947217-6-1 (Print)
       978-0-9947217-7-8 (eBook)

inspired by these 'words'

redOystor
London | Johannesburg | New York

Dedication

…to all the women who laugh AND smile to make their world a better place…

Disclaimer

This book is a collection of thoughts and quotes that have inspired the Author. Some of which may be copyrighted material. Where possible the permission of the Author has been requested with the requisite approval for the use of such content, Where it was not possible to get such permission before going to print, the copyright owner has been sighted as the originator of the quoted content.

Table of Content

Preface	1
About this book	5
...because	9
'I AM'	75
Woman!	121
...these words	151
An Epilogue	153
About the author	167

Preface

Outside of science, women alone hold the ability to recreate another human form.

That in itself is godly.

The writings that follow have been my greatest source of inspiration – there is nothing as empowering as the words of wisdom from amazing women who have been quoted throughout history.

In this book I have put together a collection of quotes, punctuated by my thoughts – that have helped me reflect on what it means to be a woman.

I share my inspiration in simple pros and quotes because I know and understand that in between your many roles of being a woman - as a daughter, a mother, a wife and a leader in business and community - you need short bursts of inspiration that take you higher into your space of achievement.

These pros and quotes have groomed my desire to be the best that I can be. And I hope they can do the same for you.

About this book

This book is simple to read. You don't have to start from the beginning or read till the end.

Open any page and you will be greeted by a burst of inspiration.

Every page is a new chapter - at least that is what I wanted to achieve.

The thoughts and quotes are presented in three sections – firstly '…because' then 'I AM' and closing with 'WOMAN'.

The thinking behind these sections is that women are many thing. Sometimes we are 'simple', other times we are 'complicated' but to the world we may appear to be 'Simply Complicated'

The quotes and thoughts of each section are a reflection of that – Simple, Complicated and Simply Complicated.

The '…because' section is very typical of what many view as what it means to be a woman – it's funny, it's *girly* and it may even be stereotypical.

'I AM' taps into a deeper connection of my thoughts. From the great 'I AM', I get to be in touch with my purpose for which I have been created. It is a reflection of the journey I have walked and the foot prints left in the sands of time - 'I AM'. With it I become that which I was meant to be. I discover myself and these words shall help you to discover who you are.

'Woman' is a section that is dear to my heart. It is a space where I get to speak to the woman in me and the women around me. Some parts are a frank conversation, others are heart to heart talk.

Remember this books is not intended to be read from start to finish, it is written with the busy woman in mind. And for that reason it is my desire that you enjoy every page, every word and every thought.

My journey is your journey, which becomes our journey. Like a girls trip to forever land, your reading this book is a creation of a lasting memory. The legacy we leave behind. And a footnote in the sands of time.

Enjoy!

If we must, I believe we can!

...because

1

"God is the best inventor ever. He took a rib from a man and created a loudspeaker."
- *Unknown*

The voice of a woman may be never be loud, but it should be heard.

The investor of life crafted you with good intention, to be the voice of reason.

And if reason dictates that we are rewarded with handbags, shoes and lots of chocolate; that voice of reason had better be on load speaker.

2

"If the world were ruled by women then there would be no war... Just a couple of nations not talking with each other."
 - *Unknown*

I don't know why we don't have more female presidents.

I personally think we can do a really great job at running governments.

It would be nice to have a Department of Facials and Manicures.

If that's what makes women happy we should have it.

Besides men love happy women. With a nation full of happy women we might just manage to breed a spices of happy men too.

I smile because I can...

Try it! It makes a frown look like crap.

3

"For most of history, Anonymous was a woman."
- *Virginia Woolf*

What's the point of calling into a radio station to remain anonymous?

It's not like you haven't told the story to a thousand other people – if you want advice, get a puppy; it may be the only form of innocent loyalty.

And why does is seem like women are the only people who have relationship problems.

Shopping makes us happy.

Can I get an 'amen' for that.

But seriously though, nothing heals an aching heart like retail therapy.

If your doctor knew what's good for you, he/she would simply give you their credit card and bill your spending to your medical aid.

And when you shop till 'you drop', we can call the medical aid company for a booking at a spa for some massage therapy and a manicure.

It's hard being a woman, you need the medical attention of a professional masseuse.

After being admitted for a couple of hours of relaxation

and spa pleasures, I think we would be fresh enough for a trip to Dubai for some recovery retail therapy.

If you agree, hit me with a **#ShoppingMakesMeHappy**

4

"Behind every woman's priceless smile is a shopping bag filled with new clothes."
- *Unknown*

Is it me, or do all the women who say all the right things want to remain 'unknown?'

Why am I quoting unknown women – this is crazy.

Let me find a woman with a name and something really good to say.

5

"Give a girl the right shoes and she can conquer the world."

- Marilyn Monroe

Sometimes all a woman needs is a closet full of shoes and a couple of handbags.

You need every colour to go with your every mood. And if your mood swings are plenty, you'll need double the number of shoes.

Just a thought

"I don't want fear of failure to stop me doing what I really care about." - Emma Watson

WOW

That is not an exclamation.

WOW… it means Woman of Wonder. You are amazing in every way.

You possess the power to create and recreate. That in itself is godly.

Woman of Wonder… Take your place; nurture the offspring of mother earth.

Tomorrow brings with it the splendor of joy, smile with great appreciation for the work you have done.

You have been torn down.

Your resilience makes me wonder… WOW.

Woman of Wonder… you are beautiful.

"I am a Woman
Phenomenally.
Phenomenal Woman,
that's me."
 - *Maya Angelou*

Now I know where we belong…

Maybe not in the heavens above but here on earth. This place is where I call home.

The here and the now is my chance to make my presence felt, enjoyed and remembered.

And when I am done… in the words of Beyoncé… many will remember:

I WAS HERE

7

"…Women ARE complicated. Women are multifaceted. Not because women are crazy. But because people are crazy, and women happen to be people."

-*Tavi Gevinson*

If I was paid for the many titles I hold, I'd have to cash a cheque every other week.

Daughter
Mother
Wife
Sister
Aunt
Boss Lady

Did someone say BOSS LADY?
That sounds phenomenal.
And that is who you are.

8

"I prefer the word homemaker, because housewife always implies that there may be a wife someplace else."

  - *Bella Abzug*

Every woman is beautiful.

You need to know that.

You don't need whistles and hoots to confirm that.

You are complete just the way you are.

A little bit of make up here and there to enhance your beauty. Every brush stroke is a touch of perfection for the wonderfully made.

Call Me Mrs....

Not because I am married, but because it is another one of my beautiful titles.

I am a queen.

I am a mother

I am a wife

I am a woman

The HHAC (the Head Home Maker in Charge), without me, the house is not a home.

Call me what you will, and still I stand my ground for who I want to be.

Identity intact, clutch bag by my side, I stroll with confidence for who I am, I was meant to be.

#WhatsYourHandle

9

"Confidence is 10 percent hard work and 90 percent delusion."

 -*Tina Fey*

Women of the South?

Inspired by the incredible country in which I live, and the miraculous history from which we come.

For those wanting a dose of inspiration to visit our shores, cast your eyes around…

I quote women of Africa

10

"Power is something of which I am convinced there is no innocence this side of the womb."

- Nadine Gordimer

You're a beautiful woman, and you can do anything you want in this life time.

[Life...]

It's a dress rehearsal.

If you get it right in practice, you'll never have to act out for a life time.

Put on your dancing shoes.

The world is your stage. Before the real audience shows up with glaring eyes, put on the best dress rehearsal the world will envy your real performance.

11

"Age is getting to know all the ways the world turns, so that if you cannot turn the world the way you want, you can at least get out of the way so you won't get run over."

- *Miriam Makeba*

I'd like to borrow the words of Whoopi Goldberg when she says:

Normal is nothing more than a cycle on a washing machine.

We're born with success.

It is only others who point out our failures, and what they attribute to us as failure.

I think I like the idea that you know who your inner self is on a daily basis, because you know.

What was good for you 25 years ago may not be good for you now.

So, keep in touch with yourself, I think that's the first ingredient for success. Because if you're a successful human being, everything else is gravy, I think.

When your mind and heart are in the right place, nothing can stop you.

12

"Your will need a lot of perseverance to keep going. No matter how prepared or smart you are, the real test is your ability to keep going."
– *Rapelang Rabana*

You don't have to be afraid of tomorrow, it will take care of itself.

Be proud of what you have accomplished today, you have tried.

You may have not achieved what you wanted to achieve, but that does not make you're a failure.

All that you can count on is, you did your best.

And that's all that counts.

13

"Failure is an opportunity to learn and to do better next time. It's part of the path to greatness, which was never meant to be smooth."

- Khanyi Dlomo

Nothing really prepares you for the road ahead, because the knowledge you have today could be obsolete tomorrow.

All that will guide you is the principles and values that shape the form of your foundation.

Believe in yourself if no one else will. You're in a wonderful time called 'NOW'.

Make it count

14

"Sometimes we feel and regret being odd balls, yet it is our uniqueness that makes us fit for our individual purpose in life."

- Thuli Madonsela

The best thing you can do for yourself is try. I know you can do it but if you're afraid – which is still okay – at least say you will TRY.

Trying means you are doing.

It is an attempt at doing but you are doing none the less.

Once the doing gets going, don't stop. Getting started is hard enough, don't let stopping get in the way of doing.

There is a lot you can accomplish when you try, because it gets you started with DOING something.

15

"Take your risks now; as you become older, you become more fearful and less flexible. And I mean that literally. I hurt my knee this week on the treadmill, and it wasn't even on."

- Amy Poehler

Your first and foremost responsibility is to use your given talents to the best of your abilities.

Like Mary Tyler Moore once said, "You can't be brave if you've only had wonderful things happen to you."

So yes, not everything will go according to plan. It's life, but remember your responsibility.

First and foremost – to use your God-given talent to pursue your dreams to the best of your abilities.

16

"You should always speak your mind, and be bold, and be obnoxious, and do whatever you want and don't let anyone tell you to stop."
- *Chelsea Handler*

Too many times we box ourselves in what we 'could' do instead of just doing what we are supposed to do – live life to the full.

Suppose you have a dream, a desire, a wish or a want, what's stopping you from going after all that you want.

Everything you want is yours for the taking, if you just do what you are 'supposed' to do.

Wanda Sykes says, "If you feel like there's something out there that you're supposed to be doing, if you have a passion for it, then stop wishing and just do it"

Everyday, life presents you with a chance to be happy. Take it.

Happiness is a choice.

I'm here today because I refused to be let my chance pass me by.

I took a chance...

I took a chance to lead a life of purpose. To ignite the dreams of many other women with a touch of inspiration.

I am where I am today, all because…

I took a chance.

Your tomorrow begins today

There are only two days in the week you should bother yourself with – today and tomorrow.

Tomorrow
– because you must plan.

Today
– because you must act on your plans

17

"The best way for us to cultivate fearlessness in our daughters and other young women is by example. If they see their mothers and other women in their lives going forward despite fear, they'll know it's possible."

- Gloria Steinem

What defines you as a woman should never be about the functions the world has dictated to you.

If you can cook, great. If you want kids, that too is an option.

But your dreams should never be the spectators to what the world deems to be your function.

"I didn't want my future to be imprisoned in my four walls and just cooking and giving birth." — Malala Yousafzai

You have a responsibility, yes – to birth and nurture the next generation of our people.

With that responsibility you are also required to live your dreams, to chase your desires, and to pursue your purpose.

All because when you nurture, you must set an example to those that look up to you.

#SmileyFace

18

"To all the girls that think you're fat because you're not a size zero, you're the beautiful one, its society who's ugly."
 - *Marilyn Monroe*

Too many women have robbed the world of their talent because they were too afraid to show up when their presence was required.

You serve no one in acting small. Your shrinking so that others may shine denies the world a great deal of talent.

The world needs you to be the beacon of hope to the hopeless, the shining start to the lost and the healing hand of laughter and joy to those in need.

Show up.

You will be amazed to discover there are people who actually need and want you to be there.

But don't do it for them, do it for yourself. Like the sands in an hour glass, every particle makes a difference.

19

"Women are the largest untapped reservoir of talent in the world."

- Hillary Clinton

You can't please everyone.

If you'd like to please everyone, try selling ice-cream, even then you are not guaranteed, but ice-cream has been known to make many people happy.

It's impossible to please everyone.

You may try, but the reality is people will always have a different view of how you should or should not be doing things.

20

"My message to women: Do what makes you feel good because there'll always be someone who thinks you should do it differently. Whether your choices are hits or misses, at least they're your own."

- Michelle Obama

If there is anything that seems to bring a woman to life, it is compliments.

Too often we wait for the world to pay us a compliment, and when they don't, we do not find joy in who we are.

Women need to compliment themselves a lot more.

Not just how beautiful they are, but also how talented and skilled they are, how successful they can be.

If the person staring back at you in the mirror is not seeing your greatness, how can you expect the world to see your value?

You are great in every way. You are talented beyond your own ability. You can be whoever you want to be, because, like any other, you are worth more than gold.

Believe

Become

#FindCourage

21

"One isn't born courageous, one becomes it."
— *Marjane Satrapi*

Courage!

Isn't that what we all need? Courage to live lives where we can fulfill our greatest potential at work and at home, as well as our potential for joy?

Here is my question for you: What are you afraid of? Where is your fear holding you back?

If we are to live and work from our sweet spot—that place of great strength and great ease—we need the courage to be authentic, to take risks, to be different.

"I AM"

22

"I don't like to gamble, but if there is one thing I'm willing to bet on, it's myself."

- Beyoncé Knowles

Jay Danzie said, 'Your smile is your logo, your personality is your business card and how you leave others feeling after having an experience with you, that is your trademark'

If there is one person that is a stranger to all of us, it is ourselves.

'For many do not know who they are.' And when you don't know who you are, you may be tempted to believe that which is said about you is who you are.

Women are very critical of themselves, "I'm too short", "I'm not tall enough", "I'm not pretty", "I'm too fat", "I'm too skinny."

All 'I AM' this or that. And never in a good light. Always in the negative.

Our thoughts influence how and what we feel about ourselves.

And if you only have negative thoughts about who you are, you're likely to have a negative perception of your abilities, your skills, and your self-awareness.

For most of my life, I have been guilty of negative self-perception. Even when my friends suggested I enter the Tammy Taylor - Mrs. South Africa pageant, I just didn't think I was good enough, beautiful enough or talented enough.

You're enough, that's all that matters.

I realize now that the glass is always full even when you think it is half empty.

You'll have half water and half air. Or three-quarters water and a quarter of air, either way, the glass always full.

If you think you are 'not enough'?

Remember, whatever 'enough' you have, is 'good enough' to get started.

When you get out of your comfort zone, you will soon realize the amazing talent you hold.

By not sharing your talent, you only rob the world the experience of discovering who you are – so 'I AM'.

'I AM' the being that was meant to be.

I AM

23

"People say that you're going the wrong way when it's simply a way of your own."
— *Angelina Jolie*

You're the only person on Earth who has direct knowledge of every thought, feeling, and experience you've ever had.

Who could possibly know you better than you?

But your backstage access to your own mind sometimes makes you the last person on Earth others should trust about it. Think of it like owning a car - Just because you've driven it for years doesn't mean you can pinpoint when and why the engine broke down.

The good news is, 'You have some unique insight into your emotional stability.'

Most women know themselves best on the traits that are tough to observe and easy to admit. Emotional stability is an internal state, so your friends might not see it as vividly as you do.

This is how you can see yourself more clearly.

ONE: If you want to really know yourself, weekly meetings don't cut it. Have a moment of self-reflection daily.

TWO: Looking into what makes you tick and writing it down can provide a useful reference. Keep a diary or more like a journal. Nothing helps you discover who you are like a 'Dear Diary' moment.

THREE: Put yourself in situations where you can't ignore feedback from multiple sources. Be conscious of what others have to say about you. Their feedback may enhance your moments of reflection.

See the world through your own eyes.

24

"People laughed at the way I dressed, but that was the secret of my success. I didn't look like anyone."

- Coco Chanel

I frequently ask myself what's the one thing that makes me stand out from other people – in all honesty, I think it is my personality. My trademark – how people feel after they have had an experience with me.

I've been safe and mundane, which I have since realized is very dangerous to my ability to influence the world.

When you are safe, fitting in or just going with the flow, you face the risk of not standing out and selling yourself short.

Being different is just one step to unlocking your true potential.

Go one step further – Be Special!

Special is personal. When every person you interact with holds a dear memory of who you are – that is special.

25

"Every girl, no matter where she lives, deserves the opportunity to develop the promise inside of her."

- Michelle Obama

I strongly believe that everyone has a natural gift or talent. Some are more obvious than others, like the ability to sing or being built for a certain sport. However, character gifts can sometimes be hard to identify, like being able to read emotions or staying calm under pressure.

Unfortunately, many people never find their hidden talents.

Some may not believe they even have a talent. Others might lack the opportunity to develop it - either by themselves or from the support of someone, like a teacher or partner, who sees and encourages that special gift to reach its full potential.

I didn't think I had what it takes to be a Mrs. South Africa participant, let alone a Top 25 Finalist.

With a little bit of a nudge and push in the right direction, I gave in to the possibility of my own hidden talents.

Any skill you possess can be turned into a real talent if you take the time to develop it and experience all aspects of it. I didn't know I had the talent to speak, but I have learned through practice that this is a real talent to cultivate.

The more you explore a talent, the more you cultivate it. You can also learn to get the most out of your talent when you surround yourself with talented people.

As the infamous Proverb says, "As iron sharpens iron, so one person sharpens another."

My friends, my family and my partner have been the sharpening iron from which my own talents have found solid ground from where they can flourish.

26

"There is no greater pillar of stability than a strong, free and educated woman. And there is no more inspiring role model than a man who respects and cherishes women and champions their leadership."

- Angelina Jolie

Without a road-map or a plan, it may be difficult to reach your destination. Not having the right tools makes it all the more difficult to get around.

The development of self through education and personal development improves self-knowledge and identity, develops talent and potential, and contributes to the realization of your dreams and aspirations.

Acquire Knowledge

As life progresses, you are guaranteed to face a variety of circumstances, changing environments, and new roles that require you to adapt. Without the right knowledge and skills, you may find yourself left behind. Value education – formal and informal.

Personal improvement fuels ongoing success, opening career doors and boosts your self-confidence.

And there is nothing more beautiful and sexy like a confident woman.

Walk tall, the hills are only there to support you.

27

"I knew what I wanted in life and I worked day and night to achieve it, and here I am."

- Tabitha Karanja

A lot of women live their lives having no clue what they want.

Just as a friendly reminder 'You only have one life, make the most out of it.'

Do things that make you happy.

Design the life you want. To do that, here are SEVEN tips to get you started:

ONE: Be selfish. If you're constantly sacrificing your time and dreams for other people, you may find yourself losing out on what is really important to you.

Remember, it's okay to put yourself first, because if you don't, no one else will.

TWO: Regret nothing. Don't feel bad for being selfish. It's okay to give your life a chance. It's time for you to live.

If you constantly regret things you did or didn't do in the past, then you won't be able to move forward.

THREE: Figure out what you need. In your time of reflection, think about what you need the most.

Is it your family? The freedom to express yourself? Love? Financial security? Or something else? It helps to know where your priorities lie.

FOUR: Figure out what makes you truly happy. There's no waste to life if you're happy living it. Your happiness is the root of your desires.

Reflect on what makes you happy. Is it traveling? Being around children? Owning a successful business? Your significant other? Financial freedom? Whatever it is, let that be your driving force.

FIVE: Figure out what bugs you. You can never be happy if your life is full of 'bugs'. Whatever bothers you, holds you back. Figure out what's holding you back, and be specific about it.

Could it be your workload? Or your meaningless job title? Whatever it is, you need to fix it – and fix it real quick.

SIX: Share your dreams. Don't keep your goals and desires to yourself. Voice them all out! If you tell people what you're trying to achieve, they will most likely support you.

SEVEN: Stay Positive. Life does not always turn out the way we want it. So don't lose heart when things don't go according to your plan. Keep trying, progress is the only way to get to your next goal post. Roll with the butterflies and buzz with the bees.

Sometimes a positive attitude is all you need to keep going.

28

"I have always believed that women can do anything they set their hearts on"

- Pam Golding

FOCUS

Stop focusing on what you don't want, instead focus on what you DO want!

I want a good job.

I want a great career

I want an amazing family

I want to travel the world

I want to be a person of influence

I want to be successful

I want to share my success with others.

Say what you want and you will get it.

29

"If you have a crazy idea, go for it! Don't be afraid to make mistakes."

- *Bethlehem Tilahun Alemu*

Just Try...

It's never easy to admit when you have made a mistake, but it's a crucial step in learning, growing, and improving yourself.

Don't be afraid to try, it is the only opportunity to learn.

Mistakes do happen, but lessons are also needed.

In the school of life, you won't get by without a Degree in 'Trial and Error'

30

"Everything is possible. Impossible just takes a little longer."
- *Wendy Ackerman*

'I AM' Possible

Everything is possible, if ... you believe.

You need to know that nothing in life has any meaning other than the meaning YOU give to it.

So if you believe... Everything is possible.

31

"My advice to women all the time is: If you want a certain future, go out and create it. Conquer your fears as that is what enslaves most women."

- Divine Ndhlukula

The future is not tomorrow. The future is everything your do today.

32

"Never listen to anybody who tells you, 'you can't do it.' You know you can so just get on with it."

- *Margaret Hirsch*

When I started this journey - from filling in the forms for taking part in the Tammy Taylor – Mrs South Africa pageant – I had no idea what to expect, fear gripped me.

It is amazing how crippling the grip of fear can be. But in the words of Nelson Mandela *(I know he is not a woman, but allow me to have just one male feature)* – 'Courage is not the absence of fear, but the triumph over it. The brave man (or WOMAN) is not (S)he who does not feel afraid, but (S)he who conquers that fear.'

SIDE NOTE: *That's it, I'm done with featuring men. They don't even bother to include us in their quotes. But you get the idea.*

Fear is a reality of human life whether we like it or not. And there is nothing wrong with fear, but you must overcome your fears to make room for the endless possibilities to your potential.

On the upside, you can also turn your fears into a source of inspiration to do more and be more in life? And here's how:

ONE: Acknowledge your fears. You cannot overcome what you have not acknowledged.

The first step to handling your fears is acknowledging what truly makes you fearful.

TWO: Embrace your mistakes. We all make mistake, but only when we embrace our wrongdoings are we able to correct where we went wrong.

THREE: Erase negative imprints. Your life experiences may leave you more 'fear-full' than 'fear-less' - a failed marriage, a lost job or a betrayal from a friend.

The way to deal with these fears is to let go of the past, it can't touch you anymore. Look forward to the future, bright is the day-after-tomorrow.

FOUR: Learn to say no. You might fear that you will disappoint someone by saying 'No'. You don't have to respond to every WhatsApp message, email or Facebook message immediately. Say no to the things that are not a priority, Say 'Yes' to those things that move you forward.

FIVE: Ask For Help. It doesn't matter who you are or what you do, at one point or another in life we all need help with something. Asking for help shows you are reasonable. Asking for help allows you to avoid the same mistakes or making mistakes others have made.

Don't let fear rule over you. You have more strength inside you then you know.

33

"The most important thing is to trust your inner instincts. Look at what you respect; who you respect and who you believe in."
- *Angela Dick*

I read a quote once and it said, 'When a woman speaks to God, she is said to be praying; but when God speaks to a woman, she is said to be CRAZY.'

I don't know who said that, but maybe I just made that up. In which case it's a good thing because now you have another woman you can quote for inspiring words.

On my way to the Tammy Taylor - Mrs South Africa casting at Emperors Palace in Johannesburg, South Africa; a billboard that grabbed my attention. It was an advertisement of a book by Francine Rivers – 'The Masterpiece'.

That word stuck with me for the duration of the casting. I could almost hear the voice in my head saying – you're a 'Masterpiece'.

I shared this with one of the ladies who was at the casting with me and she said she had seen the same billboard, and the word stuck with her too – "you're a Masterpiece."

If you will, I'd like to think that this was my moment of 'crazy'.

Voices in my head, telling me:

You're a Masterpiece.

On the second day of casting, I wore a blue dress. I've come to know the color blue to represent royalty. By sheer coincidence that day I took a picture next to a blue car. This time, the recurring voice in my head said, 'You are Royalty.'

In the words of a man I would not like to mention, because I promised Nelson Mandela would be the last – "Coincidence is God's way of remaining anonymous." Call me 'Crazy' but I know He is there.

Graceful Moments of Splendour.

Just when I thought the voices in my head had subsided, the word 'Graceful' came to mind.

This time around I stopped thinking I was 'crazy' and started listening.

For a lot of women, when you don't know you are guided, you miss the calling to your life's purpose. When you're done speaking to God, it's time you started to listen.

Embrace your moment of 'crazy' and you will discover "You're a Masterpiece of Royalty in Graceful splendour."

34

"If I can change the life of one person it makes a whole difference because behind that person there is a whole family. It's a family, it's a society, it's a nation."

- *Victoria Kisyombe*

What you do today, prepares a better tomorrow for a young generation of women leaders.

Be of influence.

35

"Have a vision and passion. Be courageous, focused and disciplined. Lastly, persist… it's definitely not easy."

- Monica Musonda

No one said it would be easy. But if you ask me, it will be worth it.

Find Courage

Stay Focused

Follow the process

36

"I am guided each day by these three questions: 'What are you fixing?' 'What are you making?' and 'Who are you helping?'"

- Juliana Rotich

Reach out and touch, somebody's hand. Make this a better place when you can.

At the end of the day, it is not always how much money you have made, how much you have accomplished or what possessions you have accumulated but how many lives you have touched.

Stretch your arm, and reach out to the next generation of heroins. Maybe not in capes and tights, but heroins none the less.

Woman!

37

"True success is about the passion to create a better world, live a life that you can look back on and be truly proud of."
 - *Dr. Ola Orekunrin*

Have you ever noticed how you mother always calls you by the name you don't like whenever you have done something she disapprove of.

As a mother I am tempted to call you 'female person' not as an insult but a call of duty. To evoke in you a sense of purpose, responsibility and duty.

This is a conversation from one woman to another.

A necessary conversation between 'me and you', about 'you and me'

Let's TALK...

38

"When the whole world is silent, even one voice becomes powerful."

- Malala Yousafzai

We've been silent to the call of duty, to take up our responsibility and embrace our purpose.

We are more than just sexual objects of desire – but we must entice the world.

We are more than breast milk and cooking pots – but we must feed the nations.

We are more than assistant help and personalized concierge – but we must guide the executive.

We serve no-one by reducing ourselves to 'function' when we can rise up to purpose. Because even a pencil has its many functions – to pick a hole, to scratch an itchy head, ear or back – its purpose remains intact; to write.

Rise up and get counted. You have no reason playing small so that others may appear large. Take up your rightful place – not ahead, not behind; not above and not below but side by side to God's human design.

39

"If I stop to kick every barking dog I am not going to get where I'm going."
- *Jackie Joyner-Kersee*

If there is anything that women do best – complaining would be it. We are professionals at it.

I know there are times when we just want to voice our frustration, not necessarily that we need or want a solution, but complaining for the sake of complaining seems to be a great past time.

Everyday, every where, we are faced with barking dogs. And if we stop to kick at everyone of them, you may lose focus on where we are headed and possibly never get to where we are going.

Stop complaining and start contemplating, complimenting and complementing.

Let us think, and speak our mind.

Let us give praise when praise is due.

Let us be the lending hand to God's human design.

Just Keep Moving

Nothing should get in the way of your progress.

40

"The question isn't who is going to let me; it's who is going to stop me."
- *Ayn Rand*

Read...

Anti-aging and anti-wrinkle creams may keep you looking young, you may need that.

However, 8 glasses of water a day with a good book to read, that will keep your mind young and your blood flowing, especially when you have to visit the loo every other hour.

Far more important than wrinkle and anti-aging cream, feed your mind with knowledge and education.

Be forever learning.

Read. Read and Read.

41

"One of the secrets to staying young is to always do things you don't know how to do, to keep learning."

- *Ruth Reichl*

...and read sum-more

Not just status updates and 140 character tweets – they have their nutritional value, but nobody should live on fast food every day.

Read solid books, attend seminars, take part in conferences, and forums – the knowledge you gain is the strength you need for progress.

You need that knowledge to create yourself a better tomorrow. And it starts with reading today.

42

"Learn from the mistakes of others. You can't live long enough to make them all yourself."

- Eleanor Roosevelt

Get Guidance...

Mentors and coaches have their purpose. And you need them. They are your earthly guides in God's human design.

Remember! You cannot make all the mistakes you need to learn the lessons in the school of life.

Those that have walked the road ahead are there to share their experiences so that you don't have to go through the same experiences.

Find someone who will walk with you, to mentor and guide your progress.

43

"You can be the lead in your own life."
 - *Kerry Washington*

You're the Star

Your life is a story. Every moment, is a scene, an act of drama and intrigue.

Like the thriller you are, many will feature, but you must still remain the lead role in the story of your life.

44

"Everyone shines, given the right lighting."
- *Susan Cain*

Let them shine

We have the responsibility to shine so that those who follow us may shine even brighter.

We have a duty to set an example that paves the path for those that seek to follow in our footsteps.

Where we can, we must guide with diligence, love and care.

46

"The challenge is not to be perfect...it's to be whole."
- *Jane Fonda*

You don't have to be perfect. Not good enough is good enough to get you started.

#MoreThanEnough

47

"There are two kinds of people, those who do the work and those who take the credit. Try to be in the first group; there is less competition there."

- Indira Gandhi

There's a sense of belonging when you know you have made your contribution to God's human design.

Act boldly, so that when you are gone, those that remain will remember

...You were here

48

"If you find someone you love in your life, then hang on to that love."

- Princess Diana

Love is...

We fall in love by chance. We stay in love by choice. And when we make that choice, our every action is an act of love.

Love is not blind, it sees all that is good and kind.

Love is boastful, it holds pride in what is dear to the heart.

Love is beautiful, it takes care of its own, with trust, hope, and perseverance.

Love is true, it never fails to honor and protect.

When angered, love is patient with understanding and forgiveness.

But love is also not stupid, it is wise to know what is and is not love.

When you find love, treasure it. When love finds you, honor it.

You have the Power to influence the world with your thoughts, words and actions.

Use it

49

"We do not need magic to change the world, we carry all the power we need inside ourselves already: we have the power to imagine better."

- J.K. Rowling

I close

There are many words that have inspired me, from Bible verses to simple quotes – some with greater impact than others.

But because I have allowed myself to embrace my moments of 'Crazy' I find that I hear the voice that guides me.

You're a miracle waiting to happen, but first, you must see the magic in your eyes.

God is able, your only responsibility is to 'respond' to His ability.

...these word

...inspire me

An Epilogue

The Wife of Noble Character (Proverbs 31: 10-31)

10 [a]A wife of noble character who can find? She is worth far more than rubies.

11 Her husband has full confidence in her and lacks nothing of value.

12 She brings him good, not harm, all the days of her life.

13 She selects wool and flax and works with eager hands.

14 She is like the merchant ships, bringing her food from afar.

15 She gets up while it is still night; she provides food for her family and portions for her female servants.

16 She considers a field and buys it; out of her earnings she plants a vineyard.

17 She sets about her work vigorously; her arms are strong for her tasks.

18 She sees that her trading is profitable, and her lamp does not go out at night.

19 In her hand she holds the distaff and grasps the spindle with her fingers.

20 She opens her arms to the poor and extends her hands to the needy.

21 When it snows, she has no fear for her household; for all of them are clothed in scarlet.

22 She makes coverings for her bed; she is clothed in fine linen and purple.

23 Her husband is respected at the city gate, where he takes his seat among the elders of the land.

24 She makes linen garments and sells them, and supplies the merchants with sashes.

25 She is clothed with strength and dignity; she can laugh at the days to come.

26 She speaks with wisdom, and faithful instruction is on her tongue.

27 She watches over the affairs of her household and does not eat the bread of idleness.

28 Her children arise and call her blessed; her husband also, and he praises her:

29 "Many women do noble things, but

you surpass them all."

30 Charm is deceptive, and beauty is fleeting; but a woman who fears the Lord is to be praised.

31 Honor her for all that her hands have done, and let her works bring her praise at the city gate.

Becoming a Proverbs 31 Woman

Nora Conrad says becoming a Proverbs 31 Woman does not mean you have to be married or have kids.

There are verses that mention how to be a good mother and wife, but preparing your heart for those things can help bring you closer to God. Working on becoming a Proverbs 31 woman is something that should be practiced daily, no matter where you are in your walk with God or in life.

WHAT DOES ALL THIS MEAN?

10- VIRTUE

The first line begins by telling women they are precious and worthwhile.

God calls us to be virtuous and capable.

11- FAITHFULNESS

We are called to speak the truth and earn the trust of others. We are to be faithful and enrich not only our lives, but the people around us as well.

12- GOODNESS

We are called to be good to our husbands and family.

To cherish them and love them.

13- HARD WORKING

God calls us to be hard workers, never lazy and always improving ourselves.

14- PROVIDER

This verse talks about providing the family with food, cooking and serving. This can be taken literally or as I see it, to care for and help your family.

15- EARLY RISER

God calls us to wake up before dawn (Maybe one of the hardest tasks for me) and prepare for the day.

I see this as God calling us to be hard working and purposeful with our time. I start my day in prayer and then preparing for the day.

16- BUSINESS SAVVY

This verse was one I had a hard time with. Many people read the Bible and think women should stay home and be housewives.

While there is nothing wrong with that, the Lord also calls on us to work hard, earn an income and help our family.

It is our job to pay attention to our world and take advantage of opportunities.

17- STRENGTH

Energetic and Strong. This can be your physical strength (working out, health), mental strength (being there for others when they need help) and spiritual strength (asking God for guidance and praying). We are called to do these things with optimism and energy.

18- ENDURANCE

Again, we are called to be hard workers. Not only that, but God asks us to ensure our dealings are well handled, even if it means staying up late. We are called to endure during hard times and to continue to work hard.

19- WELL ROUNDED

This verse was another hard one for me. I decided that because verse 13 talks about wool and flax, that this comparison calls for us to be well rounded and understanding of many skills. God calls us to learn and grow and by learning different skills we can help our family.

20- CHARITABLE

We are called to help the poor and less fortunate.

We are told to love our neighbors and this verse calls us to love those in need by welcoming them with open arms. I also think that has to do with not judging others.

21- PROVIDE AND TRUST

This verse has two key ideas.

One being it is our job to provide for our kids and family, to keep them safe and loved.

The second being trust in God and his plan. Even during hard times, trust in our work and his is key.

22- WELL DRESS

This verse in interesting.

God asks us to not be consumed by our looks, but here he tells us to be well dressed.

The idea is to treat ourselves like we are worth, which we are!

We are told to dress well to present our success that we have made for ourselves and to love ourselves.

23- WIFE TO A GOOD HUSBAND

This verse is God telling us to marry a man who is a good husband and a good leader.

There are many places that talk about marriage in the Bible. I think this verse reiterates that God calls us to marry a man with the same faith as ourselves.

Someone who loves God will be a good husband and leader.

24- WORKING

Another verse calling us to work for an income. God wants us to provide for ourselves and family. He asks us to sell our work and earn a living wage.

25- HONORABLE

This is one of my favorite verses. We are called to fear nothing but God.

We are told to be honorable and strong and to carry ourselves as graceful women. We are also told to laugh - be happy and optimistic.

26- WISE

We are asked to think before we speak and to always do so with kindness. It is asked that we be wise with what we say.

27- ACTIVE

Laziness is not an option. God calls us to take care of our homes (and families) and to work hard for them.

28- PRAISE WORTHY

We are promised thanks and praise for our hard work. We are asked to take these praises and give back to our families.

29- EXCELS

With God in our hearts, we can do and achieve anything we set our sights on.

We are told we will succeed and excel.

30- GOD FEARING

We are called to fear the Lord. He is the only one we should fear, and through that fear we will come to know him and accept him into our hearts.

We are told to live in a way that honors God.

31- REWARDED

The last verse tells us that we will be praised for our hard work and dedication. God promises to recognize our faith.

HOW TO APPLY PROVERBS 31 TO YOUR LIFE

Obviously that is a lot to take in. We are not perfect, nor does God expect us to be. Becoming a Proverbs 31 woman means working hard to become a woman who honors God.

To simplify this even more I have a list of things I try to do daily/weekly/monthly that helps me become closer to God.

- » Remember that you are worthy of God's grace.
- » Be truthful and faithful.
- » Love others, be good to others and pray for others.
- » Work hard in everything you do.
- » Wake up early and start the day with God. Pray every day and praise our Lord.
- » Study and learn. Enrich your life

with knowledge and understanding and become well rounded in your skills.

» Take advantage of opportunities in business, helping others, and caring for others.

» Be strong and endure hard times. Put your faith in God to help you when you feel lost.

» Love and honor yourself; dress well, exercise, behave well.

» Find a husband who shares your values and love of God.

» Fear God and honor him in all things.

» Remember that you are praise worthy and will be rewarded for your work.

PS: This Epilogue is an extract from Nora Conrad's Blog >> NoraConrad.com

Source: www.noraconrad.com/blog/becoming-a-proverbs-31-woman

from my
lips to
yours...

About the Author

Mrs. Vuyo Maqubela is a 'Crazy' woman of God. Crazy because she chooses to listen when God speaks.

She is a mother, a wife, a student of life and a person of influence.

She made it to the Top 100, and then the Top 25 Finalist for Tammy Taylor – Mrs. South Africa. With your help, she is 'Crazy' enough to believe she can make it to the top. This book is her journey, yours and ours.

"…because I AM woman" lets us walk with the faith that everything is possible.

Connect with Vuyo Maqubela online: **@Vuyo_Maqubela** on Facebook and Instagram.

The end…

www.ingramcontent.com/pod-product-compliance
Lightning Source LLC
Chambersburg PA
CBHW022107090426
42743CB00008B/752